You and Your Pet

Mouse

Jean Coppendale

QED Publishing

Copyright © QED Publishing 2004

First published in the UK in 2004 by
QED Publishing
A division of Quarto Publishing plc
The Fitzpatrick Building
188–194 York Way, London N7 9QP
United Kingdom

A Catalogue record for this book is available from the British Library.

ISBN 1 84538 056 8

Written by Jean Coppendale
Consultant Michaela Miller
Designed by Susi Martin
Editor Gill Munton
All photographs by Jane Burton except
page 6bl and 8cl Mayleen Snyder
page 7tc and 7r Craig Robbins, American Fancy Rat and Mice Association
page 20 vegetables by Chris Taylor
Picture of Nibbles on page 29 by Georgie Meek
With many thanks to Maddy and Angus Fitzsimmons

Creative Director Louise Morley
Editorial Manager Jean Coppendale

Printed and bound in China

Words in **bold**
are explained
on page 32.

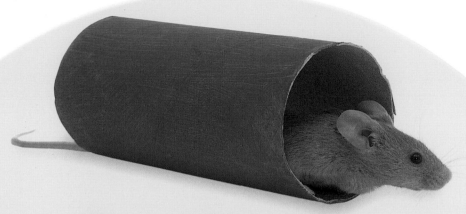

Contents

Your first mouse

Mice make great pets. They are friendly and they love to play. But mice are not toys. They are very small and fragile, and easily hurt.

Mice move very quickly, so you need to be very careful when you are handling them or playing with them. Always be gentle when you are handling mice.

Mice move very quickly and wriggle a lot, so they should not be handled by very young children or boisterous children.

Looking after an animal is your responsibility, not your child's. Try to make sure that he or she is not going to get bored with the mouse before you buy one.

▲ Mice can live for between two to three years.

◀ Mice like to play together.

Which mouse?

Some mice have short hair, and some have long hair.

◀ **A long-haired mouse will need to be brushed every day.**

Mice get lonely, so it is best to keep two or three mice together.

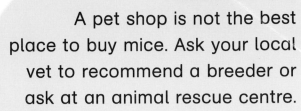
Mice are lots of fun

Choose mice that are friendly, and have bright eyes and clean, glossy fur and no lumps or skin problems.

▼ **When choosing mice, make sure they are able to run around easily.**

Lots of mice

There are lots of different **breeds** of mouse. They have different markings and colourings.

◀ **Fawn and white mouse**

Albino mouse ▼

▲ **Grey and white long-haired mouse**

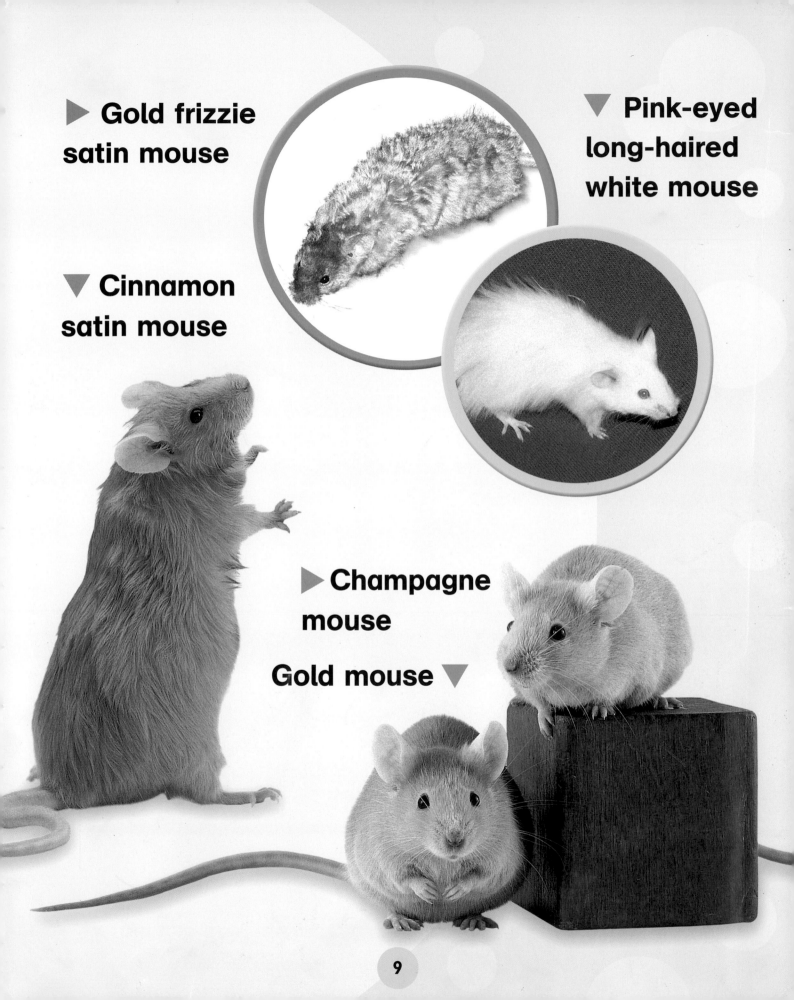

▶ **Gold frizzie satin mouse**

▼ **Pink-eyed long-haired white mouse**

▼ **Cinnamon satin mouse**

▶ **Champagne mouse**

Gold mouse ▼

Mouse shopping list

Your mice will need:

▲ **Special mouse bedding. Not cedar or pine wood shavings**

▲ **A small cardboard box filled with shredded white kitchen towel and/or hay for bedding**

◀ **A food bowl**

▶ **A water bottle with a metal spout**

▲ **Mouse food**

▼ **A tank with a secure cover**

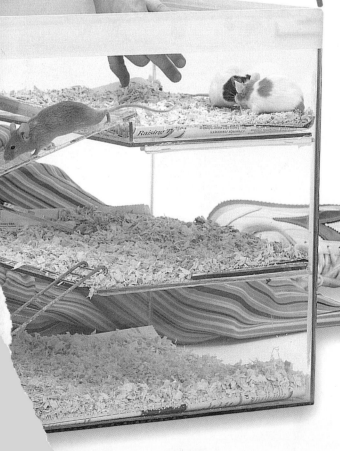

Your pet will enjoy playing with toys

▶ **A scoop for cleaning out the tank**

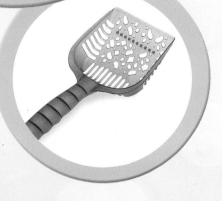

Getting ready

The best home for your mice is a glass tank, or aquarium, with a wire mesh lid – or a plastic tank.

Cover the bottom of the tank with newspaper and then put lots of special mouse bedding on top. Add some hay or torn-up white kitchen paper so your mice can make a cosy nest.

▼ Put a layer of mouse bedding over the newspaper.

▲ **Make a little bed for your mice with a box full of hay or shredded white kitchen paper.**

Saying hello

When your mice arrive, they may be feeling very scared. Place them gently in their tank, and leave them alone for a little while to get used to their new home.

Mice have poor eyesight, so don't make any sudden or jerky movements near your pets as this will scare them. They will get to know you by your voice and your smell.

▲ **Give your mice a bowl of food and a bottle of fresh water.**

After a couple of hours, put your hand gently into the tank and let the mice smell your fingers. Make sure your fingers do not smell of food – otherwise, the mice might try to eat them! Talk to your mice gently.

▲ **It may take several weeks for your mice to get used to you, so be very patient.**

Parent Points

Make sure your child knows how to handle the mice before he or she tries to pick them up (see pages 16–17).

Handle with care

Before you pick up one of your mice, gently place your hand next to it. If your pet sees a big hand swooping down on it, it will get very frightened and may bite you.

Take hold of your mouse very gently by the base of its tail and lift it out of the tank and put it straight into the palm of your other hand. Never let your mouse dangle upside-down, and never pull it by its tail.

▶ **Always sit down when you are playing with your pets.**

◀ **Stroke your mouse gently, from its head to its tail.**

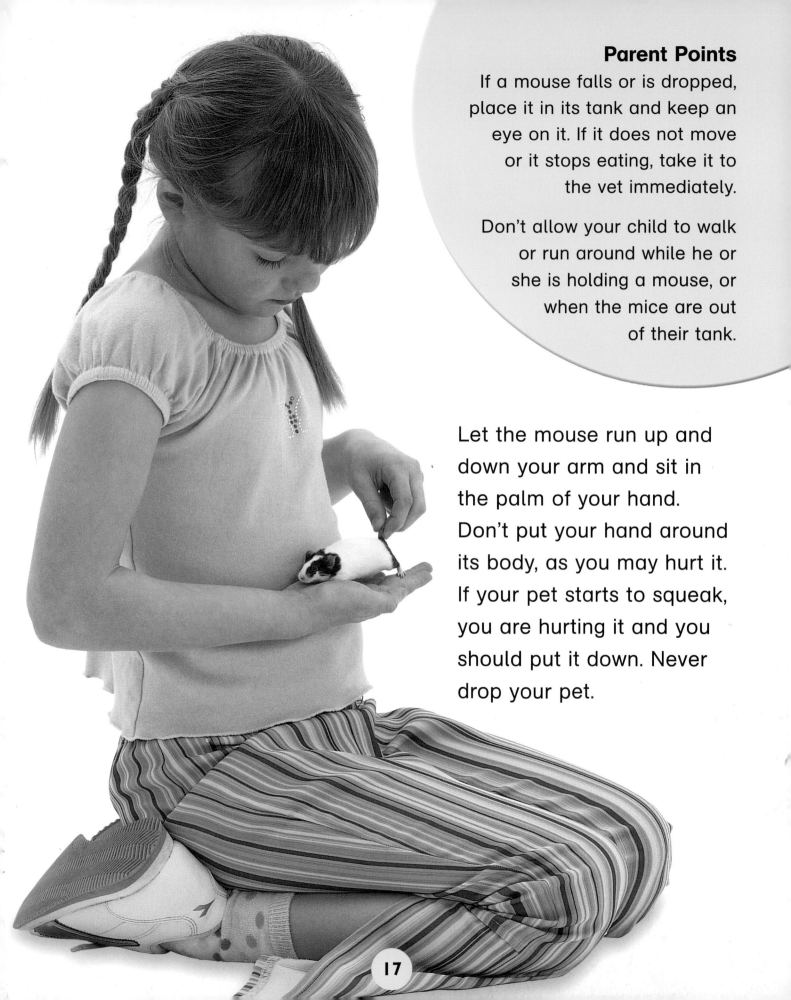

Let the mouse run up and down your arm and sit in the palm of your hand. Don't put your hand around its body, as you may hurt it. If your pet starts to squeak, you are hurting it and you should put it down. Never drop your pet.

Looking after your mice

A mouse's teeth are growing all the time, and if they grow too long it will be difficult for the mouse to eat. Give your mice a block of wood to gnaw on. This will keep their teeth short and sharp. Dog biscuits will help to keep their teeth healthy, too.

Mice love to play. Give your pets lots of toys such as toilet roll tubes and bird ladders.

Hide food in a paper bag, in a cardboard tube or under some paper for your pets to find.

▲ **If you give your mice a wheel, make sure it is a solid one, as your pets' tails or legs may get trapped in an open wheel.**

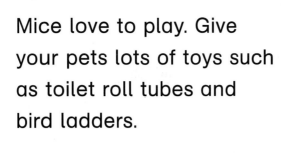

Parent Points
Mice get very few illnesses. Look out for a runny nose, eyes or bottom, or a dry, dull coat. Also, look out for any lumps or patches on the skin. If you think the mouse is unwell, take it to the vet.

If you are going to be away, you need to arrange for someone responsible to look after the mice.

Feeding your mice

Your mice should always have food available. Buy special mouse food from a petshop. You should also give them some whole or crushed oats every day.

Give your mice small pieces of fresh fruit such as apple, and vegetables such as carrots and greens, and bits of hard-boiled egg.

Cauliflower

Carrot

Broccoli

Pasta

▲ **Your mice will love a treat every now and then. Try a little boiled rice or pasta.**

Peas

▲ Make sure your mice always have plenty of fresh water to drink.

Parent Points
Never give mice cheese, lettuce, citrus fruit, sweets or chocolate, as these are bad for them.

Keep it clean

Your pets' tank or cage needs to be kept clean. Once a day, use the scoop to clear out droppings and any old bits of food.

Change the bedding every three or four days.

Give the tank or cage a good clean once a week. Clean out all the bedding and wood shavings, and wipe down the sides of the tank with animal-safe disinfectant. Wash the toys, as well.

▶ **Always wash your hands after you have cleaned out the tank or cage.**

▲ **Wash the food bowl every day. Clean the water bottle with a bottle brush once a week.**

Parent Points

Use animal-safe disinfectant (available from pet shops) for cleaning the tank. Make sure the mice are put somewhere safe while their home is being cleaned.

23

Your mouse's life cycle

▼ A female mouse can have babies when she is six to seven weeks old.

4

▶ A mouse is ready to leave its mother when it is five to six weeks old.

3

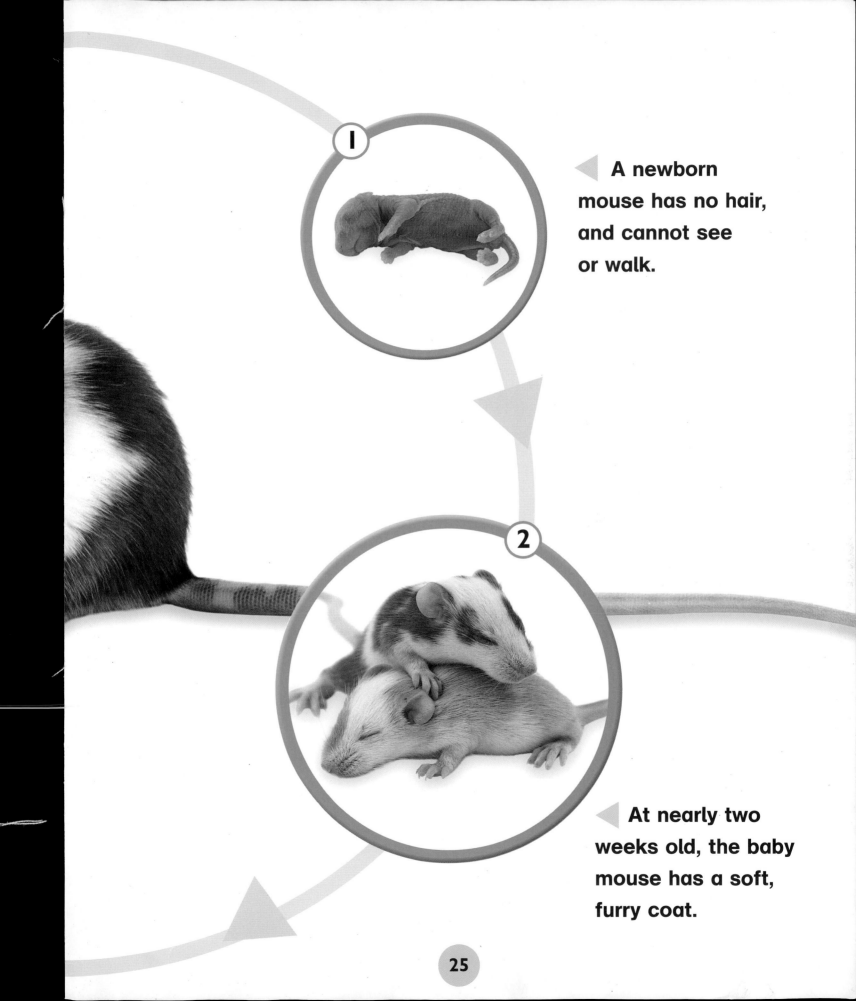

1 A newborn mouse has no hair, and cannot see or walk.

2 At nearly two weeks old, the baby mouse has a soft, furry coat.

Let's play!

You could make a playground for your mice. Put them in a big, shallow box, or make a play space for them. Make a maze out of bricks, cardboard tubes, twigs, paper bags and toys for them to explore.

Parent points
If your mice are out to play, keep them in a contained area so that they cannot disappear into corners, under doors, up chimneys, behind skirting boards or into furniture. Make sure any other pets are well out of the way.

Saying goodbye

As your mice grow older, they will play less and spend more time sleeping. Do not wake them up if they are asleep.

Nibbles last summer

◀ **Do not give your mice as much food as before, or they will get fat.**

My pet Nibbles

Keep a special scrapbook about your pet

If a mouse is very old or ill, it may die. Try not to be too sad, but remember all the fun you had together. You may want to bury your pet in the garden, but you can take it to the vet if you prefer.

Mouse checklist

Read this list, and think about all the points.

✔ Mice are not toys.

✔ Treat your mice gently – as you would like to be treated yourself.

✔ Most mice live for about two years – will you get bored with your pets?

✔ How will you treat your mice if one of them makes you angry?

✔ Never hit your pets, shout at them, drop them or throw things at them.

✔ Will you be happy to clean out your pets' tank every day?

✔ Animals feel pain, just as you do.

Parents' checklist

- **You**, not your child, are responsible for the care of the mice.

- The mice will need someone to feed them if you are away from home for more than two days.

- A mouse will only bite if it is teased with food or if it mistakes fingers for food, or if it is scared or angry.

- Mice can have a very distinctive smell.

- Mice are small pets and can easily be stepped on – make sure your child is aware of the dangers.

- Always supervise pets and children.

Mouse words

The long hairs on a mouse's face are called **whiskers**.

A mouse's fur is called its **coat**.

A mouse has claws on its **toes**.

A **breed** is a special type of mouse, such as Champagne mouse and Cinnamon satin mouse

A mouse has a long **tail**.

Index